EXPERIMENTS

WITH

TEMPERATURE

AND

HEAT

SCIENCE WHIZ
EXPERIMENTS

EXPERIMENTS WITH TEMPERATURE AND HEAT

Robert Gardner and Eric Kemer

Enslow Publishing
101 W. 23rd Street
Suite 240

Published in 2018 by Enslow Publishing, LLC.
101 W. 23rd Street, Suite 240, New York, NY 10011

Library of Congress Cataloging-in-Publication Data

Names: Gardner, Robert, 1929- author. | Kemer, Eric, author.
Title: Experiments with temperature and heat / Robert Gardner [and Eric Kemer].
Description: New York : Enslow Publishing, 2018. | Series: Science whiz
    experiments | Includes bibliographical references and index.
Identifiers: LCCN 2017001863 | ISBN 9780766086821 (library bound)
Subjects: LCSH: Temperature—Experiments—Juvenile literature. | Heat—
    Experiments—Juvenile literature. | Science projects—Juvenile literature.
Classification: LCC QC271.4 .G3654 2018 | DDC 536.078—dc23
LC record available at https://lccn.loc.gov/2017001863

Printed in China

To Our Readers: We have done our best to make sure all website addresses in
this book were active and appropriate when we went to press. However, the author
and the publisher have no control over and assume no liability for the material
available on those websites or on any websites they may link to. Any comments or
suggestions can be sent by e-mail to customerservice@enslow.com.

Illustrations by Joseph Hill

Photo Credits: Cover, p. 3, Tom Wang/Shutterstock.com; back cover and interior
pages background pattern curiosity/Shutterstock.com.

Contents

Introduction

The word "temperature" is very common to most of us. These days, we check a weather app to see what the outdoor temperature will be, and it may affect how we plan our day. Other times, the term is used to convey that someone has a fever. But temperature is an important topic in science, too, as you will discover while doing the experiments in this book.

Temperature is a basic property of any object. If the air around us is too warm or cool, we change our clothes or adjust our home thermostats. If certain foods are not kept cool, they spoil. If they are cooked at too high a temperature, they burn.

On a global scale, the temperature of the air and oceans affects the weather. Scientists are working hard to understand global warming in order to reduce its effects.

You probably sense that heat is related to temperature. Perhaps you believe that heat is something that must be added to objects to make them hotter. But what exactly is heat? Is it different from temperature?

Experimenting is how early scientists developed rules (laws of nature) and theories (explanations of the rules) about temperature and heat. With this book, you will do experiments like the ones they did. We hope your work will lead you to develop the same laws and theories.

At times, as you carry out the activities in this book, you may need a partner to help you. It is best to work with someone who enjoys experimenting as much as you do. Then you will both have fun while you are learning. **If any danger is involved in doing an experiment, you will be warned. In some cases, to avoid danger, you will be asked to work with an adult. Please do so.** We do not want you to take any chances that could lead to an injury.

Like any good scientist, you should record your ideas, procedures, data, and conclusions in a notebook. Your records will likely help you in doing further projects.

Entering a Science Fair

Some of the investigations in this book contain ideas you might use at a science fair. However, judges at science fairs do not reward projects or experiments that are simply copied from a book. For example, a diagram of different temperature scales would not impress most judges. However, finding unique ways to measure the heat needed to melt one gram of water or condense one gram of steam would attract their attention. Science fair judges tend to reward creative thought and imagination. It is difficult to be creative or imaginative unless you are really interested in your project; therefore, you should try to choose a project that you will enjoy. And before you jump into a project, consider, too, your own talents and the cost of the materials you will need.

If you decide to use an experiment or idea found in this book for a science fair, you should find ways to change or expand it. This should not be difficult. As you carry out investigations, new ideas will come to mind. And because the ideas are yours, they will be more interesting to you.

If you decide to enter a science fair and have never done so, you should read some of the books listed in the further reading section. These books deal specifically with science fairs. They will provide plenty of helpful hints and useful information that will allow you to avoid the pitfalls that sometimes trouble first-time entrants. You will learn how to prepare appealing reports that include charts and graphs, how to set up and display your work, how to present your project, and how to relate to judges and visitors.

Be Safe

Most of the projects outlined in this book are perfectly safe. However, the following safety rules are well worth reading before you start any project.

1. **Never experiment with flames or electrical appliances without adult supervision.**
2. **Do any experiments or projects, whether from this book or of your own design, under the supervision of a science teacher or other knowledgeable adult.**
3. Read all instructions carefully before proceeding with a project. If you have questions, check with your supervisor before going any further.
4. Maintain a serious attitude while conducting experiments. Fooling around can be dangerous to you and to others.
5. Wear approved safety goggles when you are working with a flame or doing anything that might cause injury to your eyes.
6. Have a first aid kit nearby while you are experimenting.
7. Do not put your fingers or any object other than properly designed electrical connectors into electrical outlets.
8. Never let water droplets come in contact with a hot light bulb.
9. The liquid in some thermometers is mercury (a dense liquid metal). It is dangerous to touch mercury or breathe mercury vapor, and such thermometers have been banned in many states. When doing these experiments, use only non-mercury thermometers, such as digital thermometers or those filled with alcohol. If you have a mercury thermometer in the house, **ask an adult** if it can be taken to a local thermometer exchange location.

Following the Scientific Method

Scientists look at the world and try to understand how things work. They make careful observations and conduct research. Different areas of science use different approaches. Depending on the problem, one method is likely to be better than another. Designing a new medicine for heart disease, studying the spread of an invasive plant, such as purple loosestrife, and finding evidence of water on Mars all require different methods.

Despite the differences, all scientists use a similar general approach in doing experiments. This is called the scientific method. In most experiments, some or all of the following steps are used: observing a problem, formulating a question, making a hypothesis (an answer to the question), making a prediction (an if-then statement), designing and conducting an experiment, analyzing results, drawing conclusions, and accepting or rejecting the hypothesis. Scientists then share their findings by writing articles that are published.

You might wonder how to start an experiment. When you observe something, you may become curious and ask a question. Your question, which could arise from an earlier experiment or from reading, may be answered by a well-designed investigation. The investigation can begin with a hypothesis. Your hypothesis is a possible answer to the question. Once you have a hypothesis, it is time to design an experiment to test a consequence of your hypothesis.

In most cases, you should do a controlled experiment. This means having two groups that are treated the same except for the one factor being tested. That factor is called a variable. For example, suppose your question is "Do green plants need light?" Your hypothesis might be that they do need light. To test the hypothesis, you would use two groups of green plants. One group is called the control group; the other is called the experimental group. The two groups should be treated the same except for one factor. Both should be planted in the same amount and type of soil, given the same amount of water, kept at the same temperature, and so forth. The control group would be placed in the dark. The experimental group would be put in the light. Light is the variable. In your experiment design, it is the only difference between the two groups.

During the experiment, you would collect data. For example, you might measure the plants' growth in centimeters, count the number of living and dead leaves, and note the color and condition of the leaves. By comparing the data collected from the control and experimental groups over a few weeks, you would draw conclusions. Survival or healthier growth of plants grown in light would allow you to conclude that to live, green plants need light.

Two other terms are often used in scientific experiments–dependent and independent variables. One dependent variable in this example is healthy growth, since it depends on light being present. That makes light the independent variable. It does not depend on anything.

After the data are collected, they are analyzed to see if they support or reject the hypothesis. The results of one experiment often lead you to a related question. Or they may send you off in a different direction. Whatever the results, something can be learned from every experiment.

Chapter 1

Measuring Temperature

What is temperature? When scientists refer to the term "temperature," they are talking about the hotness or coldness of something. It might be the air, bathwater, your food, or even your body.

Unlike people who lived a century ago, today we can control the temperature of many things. Refrigeration allows us to preserve food. Heating and air conditioning systems control the temperature of the air in buildings. No matter how cold or how hot the outside air, we can be comfortable.

In this chapter, you will do a number of experiments that will help you understand temperature and how we measure it. But first, you will find out how good you are at sensing temperature without thermometers.

1.1 Feel the Temperature

You know when it is cold. Your fingertips, toes, nose, and ears all "tell" you so. Your body senses temperature. But your body's sense of temperature can be fooled. This experiment will show you how.

1. Fill a bowl or pan about two-thirds full with cool water. Fill a second bowl or pan half-full with cool water. Then add ice cubes until it is two-thirds full. Fill a third bowl or pan two-thirds full with hot tap water. Be sure the water is not too hot to touch. If it is, wait for it to cool a bit.

hot water   cool water   ice water

Figure 1. How good are your hands at sensing temperature?

2. Place the bowls side by side, with the cool water in the middle (see Figure 1). Put one hand in the hot water and the other in the ice water. Keep your hands submerged for one minute, or until your cold hand begins to feel very uncomfortable.

3. Now put both hands in the cool water. How does the cool water feel to the hand that was in hot water? How does it feel to the hand that was in ice water? Could the cool water really have two different temperatures at the same time? Why might scientists seek to measure temperature other than by feel?

1.2 The World's First Thermometer

The great Italian scientist Galileo Galilei (1564–1642) made what may have been the world's first thermometer. It was similar to the one shown in Figure 2a. You can build one like it (Figure 2b).

1. Put the ends of two clear drinking straws together. Seal the joint by wrapping a piece of clear tape around it. (You could use a length of clear plastic tubing in place of the straws.)

2. Near one end of the straws, surround the outside with a lump of soft clay. The clay should fit around the straw snugly, but it should not squeeze it.

3. Press the clay into the mouth of a one-liter or two-liter clear plastic soda bottle. The clay should seal the mouth of the bottle.

4. Stir several drops of food coloring into a cup of water.

5. Have a partner hold the bottle upside down. Put the lower end of the straw or tubing in the colored water, as shown in Figure 2b.

6. Cover the bottle with a dish towel that has been soaked in hot tap water. Watch the end of the straw or tubing that is in

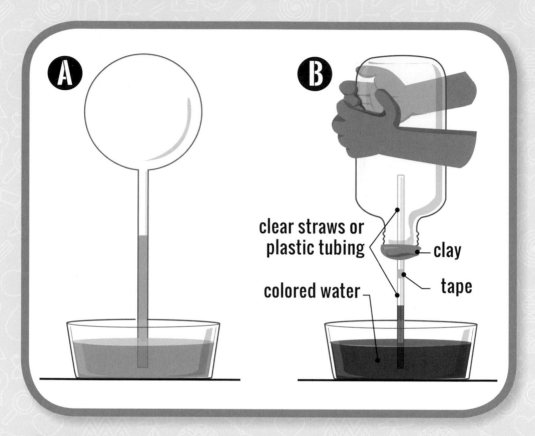

Figure 2. a) This air thermometer is similar to Galileo's. **b)** You can build your own air thermometer.

the water. What do you see? How can you tell that the air in the bottle is expanding?

7. After the air stops expanding, remove the towel. Cover the bottle with a dish towel that has been soaked in cold tap water. Watch the colored water move up the straw or tubing. Why do you think water moves up the tube?

 What happens to the water level in your air thermometer when the temperature decreases? When the temperature increases?

 How do you think Galileo used his thermometer to measure temperature?

Later Thermometers

Later, several scientists made thermometers that improved on Galileo's design. The biggest difference was that they used a liquid instead of air. It was usually alcohol or a mix of alcohol and water. They also sealed the liquid in the tube after removing the air. And they made numbered scales to measure temperature.

Alcohol thermometers limited the temperature range that could be measured. Alcohol boils at a temperature well below water's boiling temperature. Also, the volume of some water-alcohol mixtures did not change evenly with temperature.

Reliable and accurate thermometers were finally made by Gabriel Daniel Fahrenheit (1686–1736), a German scientist, in 1714. Fahrenheit used mercury, a liquid metal, in his thermometers. Mercury remained a liquid well below water's freezing temperature and well above its boiling point. In addition, mercury expanded and contracted by even amounts with changes in temperature. Fahrenheit made a scale for his thermometer. For zero degrees (the ° symbol stands for degrees), he chose the lowest thermometer reading he could get in a mixture of salt, ice, and water. For a higher temperature, he chose human body temperature, which he labeled 96°.

In measuring the density (weight per volume) of some liquids, he chose to measure them all at the same temperature: 48°. In his translated words, "I reduced it by calculation to the degree 48, which in my thermometer holds the middle place between the limit of the most intense cold obtained ... in a mixture of water, of ice, and ... sea salt, and the limit of heat which is found in the blood of a healthy man."

Later, he modified his scale to make the boiling point of water 212°. On his new scale, water froze at 32° and body temperature was 98.6°. To honor Fahrenheit, we add "degrees Fahrenheit (°F)" to his temperature scale readings.

The Fahrenheit temperature scale is widely used in the United States, but most countries and most scientists use a different scale. This other scale was invented in 1742 by a Swedish astronomer named Anders Celsius (1701-1744). Celsius's thermometer also consisted of mercury enclosed in glass. However, his scale was simpler. He labeled the freezing point of water 0° and the boiling point of water 100°. Between these two points were ninety-nine equally spaced marks. The distance between each space was one degree. Additional marks were added so that negative temperature (temperature less than 0°) and temperature greater than 100° could be measured. Today we speak of the freezing temperature of water as 0° Celsius (0°C) and its boiling point as 100°C. (Celsius first labeled the freezing point 100° and the boiling point 0°. A year later, he reversed his scale to the one we use today.)

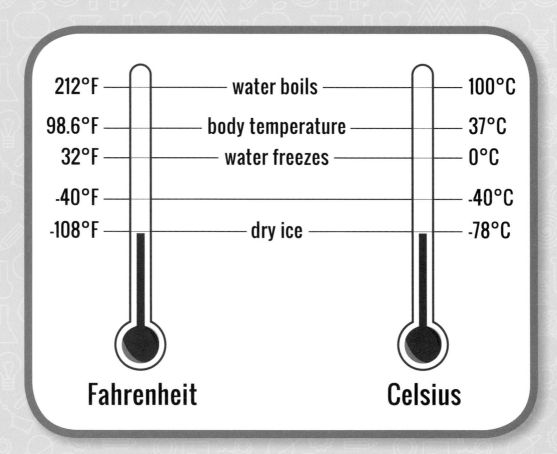

Figure 3. Fahrenheit and Celsius thermometers

For many years, Celsius's scale was known as the centigrade (one hundred steps) scale. In 1948, scientists agreed that it should be known as the Celsius scale in honor of the man who invented it. Figure 3 shows two thermometers, one having the Celsius scale and the other the Fahrenheit scale.

1.3 Celsius and a Marked Thermometer

THINGS YOU WILL NEED:

- **an adult**
- thermometer (–10 to 110°C, or 14 to 230°F)
- ice cube
- plastic cup
- crushed ice or snow
- water
- pail
- cooking pan
- a stove
- safety glasses
- oven mitt

In this experiment you will see why Celsius used boiling water and melting ice to mark his thermometer. But first you will examine the basic principle of a liquid thermometer.

1. Notice the bulb (expanded glass) at the base of a thermometer. Hold the bulb of the thermometer in your fingers. What happens to the liquid in the thermometer?

2. Place an ice cube on the thermometer bulb. What happens to the liquid in the thermometer?

As you can see, a liquid, like a gas, expands (gets bigger) when heated. It contracts (shrinks) when cooled. All liquids in glass thermometers behave this way.

Now you will see why Celsius used melting ice and boiling water to put fixed marks on his thermometer.

3. Half fill a plastic cup with crushed ice or snow. Add a little water and stir gently with a thermometer. Watch the temperature fall to 0°C (32°F).

4. Add more crushed ice or snow and stir. Does the temperature change or does it remain at 0°C?

5. Fill a pail with crushed ice or snow. Add a little water and stir with your thermometer. What do you predict is the temperature of the melting ice or snow? Check your prediction with your thermometer. What is the temperature? Were you right? Does the amount of ice or snow affect its melting temperature?

6. Half fill a cooking pan with water. **Ask an adult** to heat the pan of water on a stove at low heat. **Put on safety glasses and hold the thermometer with an oven mitt.** Put the thermometer in the water. **Do not let the thermometer touch the sides or bottom of the pan.** Watch the temperature increase as the water warms.

7. When does the temperature stop rising? What is happening to the water?

8. Watch the thermometer for several minutes. Does the temperature of the boiling water change?

Based on what you have seen in this experiment, why did Celsius choose melting ice and boiling water to determine the marks on his thermometer?

We say water boils at 100°C (212°F), but this is not always true. Under what conditions would water not boil at 100°C (212°F)?

Do an experiment to show that ice melts at the same temperature at which water freezes.

1.4 Thermometer Scale

For this experiment, you will need a thermometer without a scale. Your school may have one you can use, or you can buy one from a science supply house (see appendix).

If the thermometer has a backing on which you can make marks, move on to step one. If the thermometer has no backing, **ask an adult** to use epoxy glue to fasten it to a plastic background. Choose a piece of plastic on which you can make marks with a fine-tipped marking pen.

THINGS YOU WILL NEED:

- **an adult**
- unmarked thermometer (obtain from a science supply house or borrow from your school's science department)
- epoxy glue
- piece of plastic you can write on
- ice and water
- plastic cup
- hot tap water
- cooking pan
- a stove
- safety glasses
- oven mitt
- metric ruler
- fine-tipped marking pen
- masking tape
- watch or timer

1. Prepare a mixture of crushed ice and a little water in a plastic cup. Stir thoroughly.

2. Insert the bulb of the unmarked thermometer into the ice and water. Stir gently until the liquid inside the thermometer stops shrinking and remains at a fixed level. Use a fine-tipped marking pen to mark the level of the liquid in the thermometer.

3. Place the thermometer in hot tap water. If the liquid rises close to the top of the tube, quickly remove the thermometer. It will break if placed in very hot or boiling water. Instead, put the thermometer under your arm, between your armpit and your chest. After five minutes, remove the thermometer and quickly mark the liquid level. Record that mark as 35°C (95°F) and go to step 6. (Underarm temperature is less than body temperature, which is 37°C [98.6°F].)

4. If your thermometer can be placed in boiling water, do this rather than taking the underarm measurement. **Ask an adult** to bring half a pan of water to a boil on a stove over low heat. **Put on safety glasses and hold the thermometer with an oven mitt.** Place the thermometer bulb into the boiling water. **Do not let the thermometer touch the sides or bottom of the pan.** Wait until the liquid in the thermometer stops expanding and remains at a fixed level. **Ask the adult** to mark the level of the liquid in the thermometer.

5. You now have two fixed points on your thermometer. To make a Celsius scale, which mark will you label "0"? Which mark will you label "100"?

6. Using a metric ruler and a fine-tipped marking pen, divide the distance between the two marks into 10 equal spaces (7 if you used body temperature for the higher fixed point). How will you label these marks?

7. If possible, make further divisions. Can you make divisions above 100? Below 0?

8. If there is room, you could add the Fahrenheit scale to the thermometer. Remember that 0°C = 32°F and 100°C = 212°F. For other marks, you can convert Celsius temperature to Fahrenheit temperature using this formula:

$$°F = 1.8°C + 32.$$

For example, 20°C = 68°F, because

$$(1.8 \times 20) + 32 = 36 + 32 = 68.$$

9. You could make a scale of your own and give it your name. Cover the scale between 0 and 100 that you have just made with masking tape. Then devise your own scale.

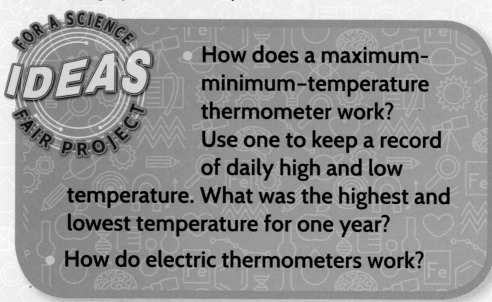

FOR A SCIENCE FAIR PROJECT IDEAS

- How does a maximum-minimum–temperature thermometer work? Use one to keep a record of daily high and low temperature. What was the highest and lowest temperature for one year?

- How do electric thermometers work?

Laws of Nature and Temperature

Fahrenheit and Celsius thermometers helped other scientists to discover some rules about temperature and heat. In science, these rules are called "laws of nature." Laws of nature allow us to predict what will happen when certain conditions exist.

But discovering laws of nature is not enough for most scientists. They want to understand why these laws work. Scientists' explanations for why the laws work are called "theories." The best theories explain many laws of nature and may even predict new ones.

As early scientists began their work, their understanding of heat and temperature was probably not as good as yours. Still, these scientists worked hard and discovered some basic rules about heat and temperature.

1.5 Temperature and Basic Laws

A Scottish chemist named Joseph Black (1728–1799) made good use of thermometers. He used them to discover some basic laws about the temperature of objects. To discover these laws he carried out many experiments. One of those experiments is similar to one you are about to do.

1. Half fill a 48-oz (1.4-L) metal can with cold tap water. Add ice cubes until the can is about two-thirds full. Stir the ice and water until the temperature is about 0°C (32°F). Then remove any remaining ice.

2. Add hot tap water to a 96-oz (2.7-L) metal can or cooking pan until it is about one-third full.

3. Set up a data table in your notebook like the one shown in Table 1.

4. Put a thermometer in each can. Record the temperature of the water in each can.

5. Put the can with the cold water into the can or pan with the hot water (see Figure 4).

6. Measure the water temperature in both containers at one-minute intervals. Record those temperature readings in your data table. Between temperature readings, gently swirl the cold-water can in the hot water. Continue recording until the temperature in both containers stops changing.

TABLE 1

Data for Experiment 1.5

Time (minutes)	Temperature	
	Hot Water	Cold Water
Start		
1		
2		
3		
4		

How did the final temperature of the water in the small can compare with the final temperature of the water in the big can or pan? Write a rule that describes what you found by doing this experiment.

Joseph Black did a number of similar experiments. He concluded, "We must therefore adopt, as one of the most general laws of heat, that all bodies communicating freely with one another ... acquire the same temperature."

Does your rule agree with Joseph Black's conclusion?

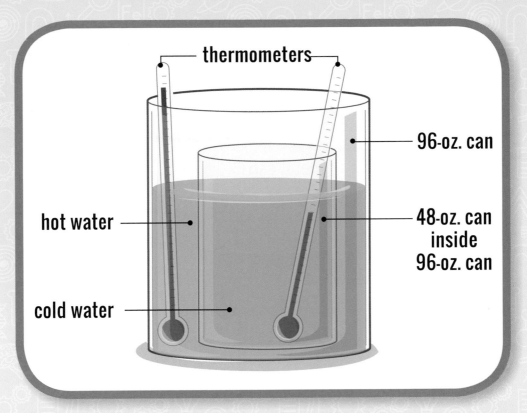

Figure 4. What happens to temperature when a small can of cold water is placed inside a larger can of hot water?

1.6 More Laws About Temperature

Suppose you put hot water in the small can and ice-cold water in the large can or pan. What do you think will happen? Use the rule you found in Experiment 1.5 to make your prediction.

1. Repeat Experiment 1.5, but this time put hot water in the small can and cold water in the big can or pan. Was your prediction correct?

2. Examine the data tables from both experiments. When did the temperature of the hot water change fastest? When did the temperature of the cold water change fastest? When did the temperature of the hot water change at the slowest rate? When did the temperature of the cold water change at the slowest rate? Does the rate at which the temperature changes depend on the difference in temperature between the hot and the cold water? Write a rule about the rate at which the temperature changes.

3. Repeat Experiment 1.5. This time put the cold water and ice in a much smaller 16-oz (0.5-L) metal can. Remove the ice after the temperature reaches 0°C (32°C).

In this experiment, a smaller amount of cold water will be warmed by the same amount of hot water, as before. Try to predict how the final water temperature in the two cans will compare with the final temperature you found in Experiment 1.5.

Was your prediction correct?

4. Repeat Experiment 1.5 once more. This time put the hot water in a 16-oz (0.5-L) metal can and the cold water in the 96-oz (2.7-L) can. Try to predict how the final temperature of the water in the two cans will compare with the final temperature you found when cold water was in the 16-oz (0.5-L) can.

Was your prediction correct?

Write a rule to explain how temperature change depends on the amounts of hot and cold water used.

Temperature Change Rules

Joseph Black arrived at rules (laws) of temperature change like the three below. Are these rules similar to the ones you came up with?

(1) When objects at different temperatures are in contact, the cooler one gets warmer and the warmer one gets cooler until their temperatures are equal.

(2) The larger the temperature difference between two objects in contact, the faster their temperatures change.

(3) The greater the amount of something, the greater the temperature change it can cause in another object, and the less its own temperature changes in the process.

Here are some things about the real world that these rules tell us:

Rule 1 tells us that objects cannot become hotter or colder than the objects they are touching. An egg in boiling water never gets hotter than 100°C (212°F), the temperature of boiling water. Rule 1 also explains how a thermometer measures temperature. It reaches the same temperature as whatever it is in. However, Rule 3 says that the thermometer should weigh much less than the object whose temperature it is measuring. If not, the thermometer will change the object's temperature quite a lot. Rule 2 tells us that to cool something quickly, put it in something that is much colder, such as ice or some other cold place.

What else about the real world do these rules tell you?

Make a Graph

Often, a useful way to display data is to make a graph. When the author did Experiment 1.5, he recorded the data shown in Table 2. A graph of his data is shown in Figure 5. Temperature is on the vertical axis. Time is on the horizontal axis. The points on the graph were connected with a smooth curved line. This allows you to find the temperature between the points on the graph that indicate actual measurements. We assume that temperature changes bit by bit between the times it is measured.

TABLE 2
Author's Data for Experiment 1.5

Time (minutes)	Temperature (°C)	
	Hot Water	Cold Water
Start	52	0
1	38	15
2	31	23
3	29	26
4	27	27
5	27	27

On the graph, an upward-sloping curve shows that the temperature was increasing. A downward-sloping curve shows that the temperature was decreasing. The steeper the curve, the faster the temperature was changing. A horizontal line indicates the temperature was not changing; it was constant.

How does the graph illustrate the first two rules of temperature change?

Plot graphs of temperature versus time for each of the four experiments you did with the cans of hot and cold water. How do the graphs illustrate all three rules of temperature change?

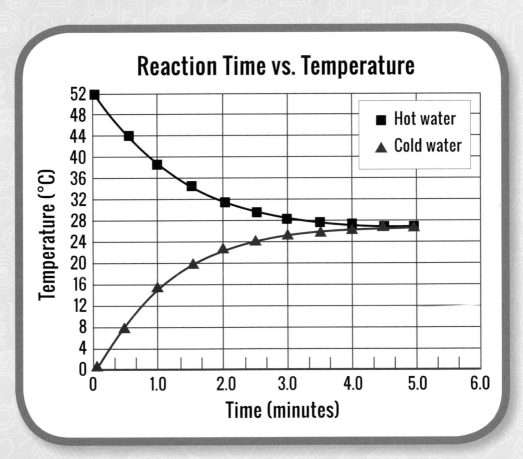

Figure 5. A graph of temperature versus time when hot and cold objects are in contact

Temperature Change and Heat

How do we explain these three rules of temperature change? That is, can we come up with a theory of temperature change? One way to form a theory is to find a familiar process that follows similar rules. We can then explain temperature change by saying it is like this other process.

Explaining one thing by showing it is like another is common in science. For example, an early theory of light compared its behavior to water waves. More recently, scientists have tried to understand the human brain by comparing it to a computer.

In the following investigation you will see that water flowing between connected containers follows a similar pattern to temperature change. We can use this similarity to build our theory of temperature and heat.

Water Levels and Temperature

THINGS YOU WILL NEED:

- **an adult**
- finishing nail or metal drawing compass point
- 2 large plastic buckets with straight sides
- sharpened pencil
- tall, narrow plastic cup or bottle with straight sides
- plastic drinking straw
- ruler
- permanent marker
- clay
- clothespin or large paper clip
- water
- clock or watch with a second hand
- a partner
- notebook
- pen or pencil

1. **Ask an adult** to help you use a nail or drawing compass point to make small holes in the sides of the two plastic buckets. Make the holes 2 cm (3/4 in) from the bottom of each bucket. Punch a hole in a similar place in a plastic cup or bottle.
2. Enlarge the holes by gently pushing and twisting a sharpened pencil into them. Make the holes about the same size as a plastic drinking straw.
3. Use a ruler and a permanent marker to draw a vertical depth scale on the sides of the containers. Make the 0 cm mark at the top of the holes. Make centimeter marks up the side to 10 cm. Label the two buckets #1 and #2 (see Figure 6a).

4. Insert the ends of a plastic drinking straw into the holes in buckets #1 and #2. Push clay around the sides of the straw where it enters the buckets to make a watertight seal.

5. Clamp the middle of the straw with a clothespin or large paper clip, and fill bucket #2 with water to the 0-cm level. Fill bucket #1 to the 10-cm mark.

6. Release the clothespin, and begin timing the water flow using a clock or watch with a second hand. As the water flows from bucket #1 into bucket #2, measure the two water levels every thirty seconds.

7. Copy Table 3 into your notebook, and record the results. Then draw a water level vs. time graph, with water level on the vertical axis and time on the horizontal axis.

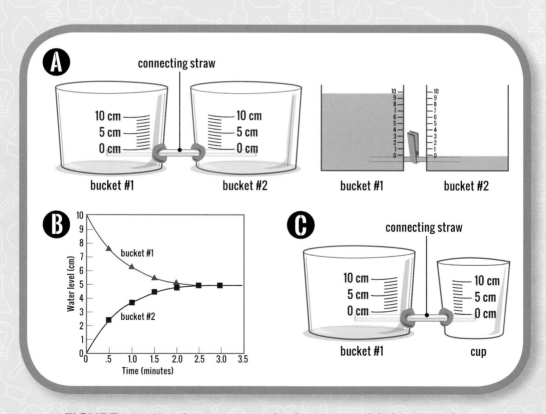

FIGURE 6. Use changing water levels as a model for the rules of temperature change.

Look at your graph. How does it compare with the one the author made for this experiment (Figure 6b)? How do the final water levels in the two buckets compare? When did the water levels change at the fastest rate? At the slowest? How does the rate at which the water levels change depend on the difference in levels? Can you write rules that describe this behavior?

TABLE 3

Water Depth vs. Time for Two Buckets

Time (minutes)	Water Depth (cm)	
	Bucket #1	Bucket #2
0	10	0
0.5		
1.0		
1.5		
...		

8. Repeat the experiment using the narrow plastic cup or bottle in place of bucket #2 (see Figure 6c). Record your results in a new table and graph. Are the final water levels in the narrow cup and larger bucket equal? How do these final levels compare to those reached when two larger buckets were used? Can you write a rule that describes how changes in water levels depend on the size of the connected containers?

9. Repeat the experiment. This time let water flow from a height of 10 cm in the narrow bottle into a water level of 0 cm in the larger bucket. Can you predict what the final water levels will be? Try the experiment. Are your results close to your prediction?

Based on the results of this experiment, can you write three rules of changing fluid levels that follow the pattern of Joseph Black's rules of temperature change listed on page 30?

Fluid Theory of Heat

Notice the similarities in the rules of water-level changes found in this experiment with the rules of temperature change on page 30. These similarities can be used to build a theory of temperature change and heat. The first step is to see that changes in temperature are like changes in fluid level. Changes in fluid level are caused by the flow of fluid. We can imagine that changes in temperature are caused by the flow of a different type of fluid. We may call this "fluid" *heat*. The greater the amount of heat added to or taken away from an object, the greater its temperature change.

It was Joseph Black who came up with an early fluid theory of heat. His theory was based on ideas like ours. Black proposed that heat is made up of very small fluid particles. The particles can move around in the spaces between the particles of normal matter. Black further proposed that bits of heat fluid are attracted to normal matter and are repelled (pushed apart) by each other.

According to this theory, temperature is a measure of how crowded together the heat particles are in an object. As more heat enters an object, the heat particles become more closely packed. The closer the packing, the higher the temperature. Adding more water to a container raises the water level. Similarly, adding more heat to an object raises its temperature.

Temperature measures how crowded the heat is, not the total amount of heat. A large cold object can have more heat in it than a small hot object. Similarly, a wide container filled to a shallow level can have more water in it than a narrow test tube filled to its brim.

Black's theory can readily explain the three rules of temperature change. The heat fluid moves from regions where it is crowded to places where it is less crowded. It moves until it is at the same level of crowding throughout. To help you understand this better, write down the three rules of temperature change in your notebook. Then, with the help of a partner, write explanations for each rule. Imagine that you are Joseph Black himself and you are determined to convince other scientists.

Chapter 2

Heat and Temperature

You now know that heat and temperature are related. But what exactly is the difference between these two things?

According to Joseph Black's theory, temperature measures how crowded heat fluid is in an object. Temperature is not the total amount of heat in the object. A large object can contain more heat than a small object at the same temperature. And a large cool object can hold more heat than a small hot object. This is similar to a large bucket filled one inch deep that holds more water than a test tube filled six inches deep.

These ideas make the difference between heat and temperature clearer. In this chapter you will do some experiments that helped early scientists understand this difference.

2.1 The Difference Between Heat and Temperature

THINGS YOU WILL NEED:

- 2 medicine cups (30-mL [1-oz])
- water
- freezer
- measuring cup
- hot tap water
- 4- to 6-oz (120- to 180-mL) plastic cup
- cold tap water
- 1-quart (1-L) plastic container
- drinking straws
- ice cubes
- thermometer (–10 to 110°C or 14 to 230°F)
- 2 foam cups (12-oz, or 350-mL)
- eyedropper

Joseph Black and others were confused about the difference between heat and temperature. To better understand the difference, they did experiments that involved melting ice. One question they asked was similar to: "Will an ice cube melt faster in a small amount of hot water or in a large amount of cold water?" They did experiments like the ones you are about to do. The experiments showed them that heat is not the same as temperature.

1. Fill two medicine cups to the 30-mL (1-oz) line with water. Put the cups in a freezer overnight.
2. Using a measuring cup, get 30 mL (1 oz) of hot water from a faucet. Pour the water into a 4- to 6-oz (120- to 180-mL) plastic cup.
3. Get 600 mL (20 oz) of cold water from a faucet. Pour it into a 1-quart (1-L) plastic container.

4. Remove the two identical pieces of ice from the freezer. Pop them out of the medicine cups. At the same time, put one piece into the hot water and the other piece into the cold water. Use separate straws to slowly stir the water in both containers. Which piece of ice melts first? Which water must have held more heat? Why did it make sense to stir the water?

5. Half fill a 1-quart (1-L) plastic container with cold water. Add ice cubes until the container is about two-thirds full. Stir the ice and water with a thermometer until the water's temperature is 0°C (32°F) or nearly so. Remove any remaining ice.

6. Add the ice water to a large (12-oz [350-mL]) foam cup until it is about half full. Be sure there is no ice in the cup.

7. Half fill a second large foam cup with hot tap water.

8. Measure and record the temperature of the hot water and the cold water. Leave the thermometer in the cold water.

9. Using an eyedropper, add one drop of the hot water to the half cup of cold water. How much did one drop of hot water change the temperature of the cold water?

10. Add ten drops of the hot water to the half cup of cold water. How much did ten drops of hot water change the temperature of the cold water?

11. Pour all the remaining hot water into the cold water. How much did the remaining hot water (nearly half a cup) change the temperature of the cold water?

Based on these two experiments, what makes you think that temperature is not the same as heat?

- Place identical ice cubes in equal volumes of water at different temperatures. Does the temperature of the water affect an ice cube's melting time? Come up with a theory to explain your results.

- Place identical ice cubes in different volumes of cold water of the same temperature. Does the amount of water affect an ice cube's melting time? Come up with a theory to explain your results.

- Find ways, besides using a cold place, such as a freezer or refrigerator, to keep an ice cube as long as possible. You might challenge classmates to an ice-cube-keeping contest. Who can keep an ice cube from melting the longest?

- Make ice of different shapes (cube, sphere, tall cylinder, flat cylinder, cone) from the same amount of water. Which shape do you think will melt fastest? Slowest? What makes you think so? Come up with a theory to explain your results.

2.2 Temperature Mixes

THINGS YOU WILL NEED:

- a partner
- 2 thermometers (–10 to 110°C or 14 to 230°F) that read very nearly the same temperature when placed side by side in a glass of water
- 1-gallon (4-L) container
- water (hot and cold)
- ice cubes
- graduated cylinder or metric measuring cup
- 2 small (6- or 7-oz [180- or 200-mL]) foam cups
- notebook
- pen or pencil
- 2 large (12-oz [350-mL]) foam cups

Early scientists did experiments to see what happens when things at different temperatures come in contact. One experiment involved mixing equal and unequal amounts of water that were at different temperatures. You can do such experiments quite easily. In fact, you have an advantage over early scientists because you can obtain insulated (foam) cups. Liquids in foam cups change temperature more slowly than in the glass or metal containers early scientists used.

Rather than weighing the water on a balance, you can measure volumes. Since one milliliter (mL) of water weighs one gram (g), 100 mL of water weighs 100 g.

1. Add cold water to a 1-gallon (4-L) plastic container until it is about half full. Then add ice cubes until it is about two-thirds full. Stir the mixture until the temperature of the ice water is 0°C (32°F) or close to it. Remove any remaining ice.

2. Add 100 mL of the ice water to a graduated cylinder or a metric measuring cup. Pour the 100 mL of ice water into a 6- or 7-oz (180- or 200-mL) foam cup. **Be sure there is no ice in the water.** At the same time, have a partner carefully add 100 mL of very hot tap water to a second foam cup.

3. Measure the temperature of your ice water. Meanwhile, your partner will measure the temperature of the hot water with the other thermometer. Quickly record both temperature readings in your notebook.

4. Pour the hot and cold water together into a 12-oz (350-mL) foam cup. Stir the 200 mL of water with a thermometer. Record the temperature when it stops changing.

   What is the temperature of the mixture of hot and cold water? Is the temperature of the mixture close to the average temperature of the hot and cold water? For example, the average temperature of 0°C and 50°C would be:

   $$\frac{50°C + 0°C = 25°C,}{2}$$

   or midway between the hot and cold water temperatures.

   Was the temperature of the mixture very close to the average temperature (midway between the hot and cold water temperatures)?

5. Measure and record the temperature of 100 mL of the ice water and 50 mL of the hot water. Pour these volumes of hot and cold water together into a large foam cup. Remember your rules about temperature change. Can you predict the temperature of the 150 mL of water after mixing? Record the temperature when it stops changing. Was your prediction correct?

6. After measuring and recording their temperature, mix 50 mL of the ice water with 100 mL of the hot water. What can you predict about the temperature of the 150 mL of water after mixing? Record the temperature when it stops changing. Was your prediction right?

7. After measuring and recording their temperature, mix 75 mL of the ice water with 100 mL of the hot water. Record the temperature when it stops changing.

8. After measuring and recording their temperature, mix 100 mL of the ice water with 75 mL of the hot water. Record the temperature when it stops changing.

You have mixed a lot of hot and cold water. (Joseph Black mixed much more.) From the results of all these experiments, can you come up with a rule or formula that will enable you to predict the temperature of any mixture of hot and cold water? (Hint: Think about the changes in temperature of the hot and cold water.)

Heat Rules

From mixing and other experiments, early scientists came to a conclusion. They concluded that heat involves the mass of something as well as its temperature. One hundred grams of water at 20°C contains more heat than a drop of water at the same or even a much higher temperature. Temperature indicates the degree of hotness of an object. But heat involves both temperature and mass.

Early scientists also concluded that heat is conserved. This means that heat is not lost. It may move from one object to another, but the heat lost by one object is gained by another object or objects. The heat lost by 100 mL of hot water at 50°C when mixed with 100 mL of cold water at 0°C is gained by the cold water. Scientists arrived at this conclusion because the temperature of the mixture was 25°C, or nearly so.

The heat transferred from one object to another can be written as an equation:

heat lost = heat gained.

They found that the number that remains the same is the mass of water multiplied by the temperature change:

mass of cold water × its change in temperature =
mass of hot water × its change in temperature.

Water expands when heated. Design an experiment to show how much water expands per degree increase in temperature.

2.3 **A Measure of Heat**

Early scientists were uncomfortable with the idea that heat is invisible and weightless. They saw this as a problem for future scientists to solve. Their mixing experiments helped them see that they could measure heat without seeing or weighing it. Heat could be measured by including both mass and temperature change.

French chemist Antoine Lavoisier (1743–1794), known as the father of modern chemistry, furthered the fluid theory of heat. He named heat fluid caloric. During his lifetime, the fluid theory of heat became known as the caloric theory. The caloric theory was eventually replaced by a new theory; however, "caloric" remains in the word calorie, which is a unit used to measure heat.

A calorie is the quantity of heat gained or lost when the temperature of 1 g of water changes by 1°C. If the temperature of 100 g of water changes from 10°C to 20°C, the heat added to the water is 1,000 calories because:

$$100 \text{ g} \times (20°C - 10°C) = 100 \text{ g} \times 10°C = 1{,}000 \text{ calories.}$$

Notice that it is through the multiplication of the mass of water by its temperature change that heat can be measured in calories.

In this experiment, you will simply return to your results from Experiment 2.2. You will apply the idea of a calorie to that data to see whether heat was conserved.

Look at the data you collected in Experiment 2.2. You used water in those experiments. Since one milliliter of water weighs one gram (1 mL = 1 g), you can consider the volumes, which you measured in milliliters (mL), to be grams.

Use that data to compare the heat lost and gained in each mixing experiment you did. For example, suppose that when you mixed

100 g of water at 50°C with 100 g of water at 0°C, the temperature of the mixture was 25°C. The heat gained by the cold water was:

100 g × (25°C – 0°C) = 100 g × 25°C = 2,500 calories.

The heat lost by the hot water was:

100 g × (50°C – 25°C) = 100 g × 25°C = 2,500 calories.

In this case, the heat lost equals the heat gained. Is this true or nearly true for the other mixtures of hot and cold water that you tested?

To find out, calculate the heat lost and heat gained for each mixture. What do you conclude?

Chapter 3

Conduction and Convection

Scientists, including Antoine Lavoisier, were curious about caloric. If it was indeed real, it was certainly a very strange substance. It could not be seen and it had no measurable weight. In fact, Lavoisier, using sensitive scales, found temperature had no effect on weight.

Strange as it was, caloric provided a good explanation of the rules of temperature change and thermal expansion. Therefore, the caloric theory became widely accepted.

Another property of heat that puzzled early scientists was its movement. In the following experiments, you will investigate the different ways that heat can move. Keep in mind that you never see caloric. You can only imagine how it moves by observing changes in temperature.

3.1 Solids and Heat Conduction

THINGS YOU WILL NEED:

- block of wood
- cloth towel
- metal pan
- counter or table
- clock or watch
- wooden cutting board
- freezer
- hot tap water
- wooden bowl, such as a salad bowl
- small metal cooking pan
- glass cooking pan
- large bucket or basin
- ice
- cold tap water
- thermometer (–10 to 110°C or 14 to 230°F)
- metal can
- notebook
- pen or pencil
- glass jar
- 2 foam cups, one with a foam cover
- graph paper
- graduated cylinder or metric measuring cup
- paper cup
- plastic cup

1. Place a block of wood, a cloth towel, and a metal pan on a counter or table. Leave them there for about twenty minutes. How would you expect the temperature of these three objects to compare? Remember the rules of temperature!

2. Touch each of the three objects. Does any one of the three feel colder than the others? But can it really be colder? If not, how can you explain what you feel?

The movement or flow of heat along or through a substance is called thermal conductivity, or simply heat conduction. The greater the thermal conductivity of a substance, the faster heat flows through it.

3. Place a metal pan and a wooden cutting board in a freezer. After about twenty minutes, remove the metal and wooden objects from the freezer. Hold one in each hand. How can you tell which material is the better conductor of heat? Which one conducts heat faster from your hand?

4. Fill a wooden bowl, such as a salad bowl, with hot tap water. Also, quickly fill a small metal cooking pan and a glass cooking pan with hot tap water.

5. Empty the wooden bowl and turn it over. Place your hand on the dry bottom of the bowl. Repeat the procedure for the metal and glass cooking pans. Which of the three solids best conducts heat to your hand?

   Substances that conduct heat well are called thermal conductors. Which of the substances you tested–wood, glass, or metal–would you call a thermal conductor? Which would you classify as a thermal insulator?

6. You can investigate heat conductivity in a more quantitative way. Fill a large bucket or basin to a depth of about 5 cm (2 in) with a mixture of ice and cold tap water. Then fill a smaller metal can with hot tap water and measure its temperature. Put the can of hot water into the ice water. Use a thermometer to measure the temperature. Record the temperature of the hot water every minute until it reaches 10°C (50°F). Record the temperature readings and times in a table.

7. Repeat the experiment using a glass jar with the same amount of hot water at the same initial (starting) temperature.

8. Perform the experiment a third time with the hot water in a foam cup.

9. Plot a graph of temperature versus time for each container. You can plot all three sets of data on the same graph. Examine the three curves on the graph. Which material is the best conductor of heat? Which is the worst conductor (or the best insulator)? Would you want to drink hot cocoa from a steel cup? Why or why not?

10. Put 100 mL of hot tap water into each of five different containers—a metal can, a paper cup, a plastic cup, a foam cup, and a foam cup with a foam cover. (The cover should have a hole so that a thermometer can go through it.) Place all five cups side by side. Measure the temperature in each cup at two-minute intervals. Plot temperature and time for each cup. Plot all the curves on the same graph.

   In which cup did the water cool fastest? Slowest? Which material is the best insulator? Does a cover affect the rate at which a liquid cools?

3.2 Liquid and Gas Conductivity

Are liquids good conductors of heat?

1. To find out, let a piece of ice slide to the bottom of a test tube. Slowly slide a metal washer or nut down the tube to hold the ice in place. Then add cold water to the test tube until it is about two-thirds full. **Ask an adult** to hold the test tube with a clamp. He or she should heat the water at the upper end of the test tube with a candle, alcohol burner, or Bunsen burner (see Figure 7a). Does the ice melt before the water boils? What does this experiment tell you about the conductivity of water?

2. As you might suspect, gases are also poor conductors of heat. You can demonstrate the poor conductivity of air. Use an aluminum soda can and an aluminum can with a flat base. The bottom of the aluminum soda can should not be flat. It should have a dome-like base. The dome provides an air pocket above whatever the can is resting on. The other aluminum can

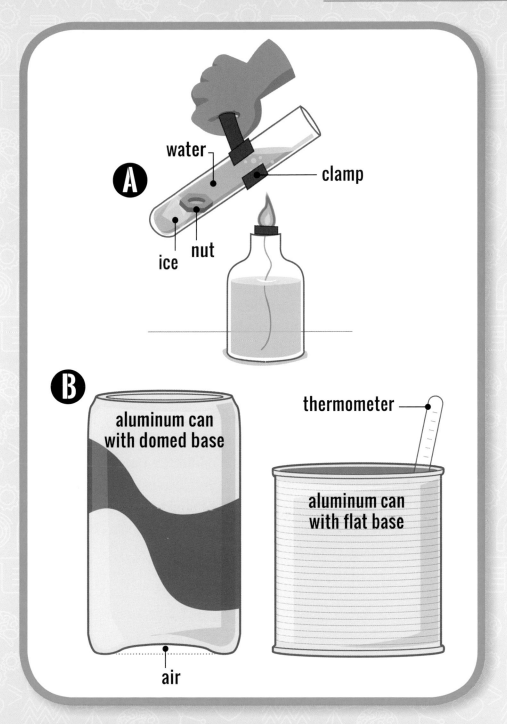

Figure 7. a) Testing heat conduction of a liquid. b) Testing heat conduction of a gas (air).

should have a flat bottom (see Figure 7b). The two cans should have very nearly the same mass. If one can is lighter than the other, line it with aluminum foil until they both weigh the same.

Pour 100 mL of cold water into both cans. The temperature of the water in the two containers should be the same.

3. Put both cans in a heavy frying pan. Place the frying pan on a stove. **Ask an adult** to heat the pan on low heat.

4. **Put on oven mitts.** Use the thermometer to occasionally stir the water in the cans. When the water temperature in the can with a flat base reaches approximately 40°C (105°F), turn off the stove.

5. Remove both containers from the frying pan and place them on a wooden cutting board. Stir the water in both containers and record the final temperature readings. Which container received more heat by conduction? How do you know? How can you account for the difference?

Does the fact that gases do not conduct heat very well seem strange? One might suppose that because gas has such a low density, it should be much easier for heat fluid to flow through it. Lavoisier and other scientists were already hypothesizing that the difference between solids and gases was the distance between particles (molecules). In a solid, atoms are packed close together; in a gas, they are far apart. Therefore, it seems that heat fluid should flow more easily through a gas. We will return to this problem in a later chapter.

Make some flat pieces of ice by freezing water in wide shallow plastic dishes or trays. Place some of the following objects on the surface of the ice: a stack of coins, a marble, a small block of wood, an eraser, a stack of metal washers, a stack of rubber washers, a plastic block, a piece of chalk. Which objects do you think will sink into the ice? Why?

3.3 Liquids and Convection

When one region of a gas or liquid gets warmer than a neighboring region, it expands. Its density (weight divided by volume) becomes less than that of its surroundings. This causes it to rise through its surroundings, carrying its heat with it. This form of heat motion is called convection. You can observe convection in a liquid.

1. Fill a clear cup with hot tap water. Add several drops of blue food coloring and stir.

2. Fill a large, clear jar or bowl with cold tap water.

3. Remove the rubber bulb from an eyedropper. Submerge the eyedropper tube in the hot colored water. When the dropper is full, place your finger firmly over the top end of the tube and remove it from the water. Keep your finger tightly pressed on the tube so the colored water will not drain out (Figure 8a).

4. Keeping the dropper upright, submerge it almost to the bottom of the jar of clear, cold water. Remove your finger from the tube (Figure 8b). From which end of the dropper does the hot colored water come out? Can you explain why?

5. Repeat this experiment with cold colored water in the dropper and hot water in the large jar or bowl. What differences do you observe?

6. Finally, repeat the experiment with the colored water at the same temperature as the surrounding water.

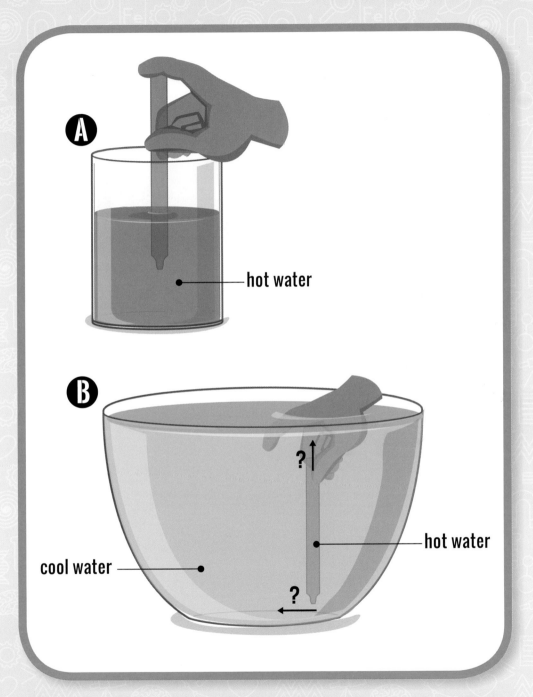

Ⓐ

hot water

Ⓑ

cool water

?

?

hot water

Figure 8. a) Remove hot water with a tube. b) Will the colored hot water move up or down?

Convection is a very common and important process in nature. On a sunny day, air over warm land near the ocean is heated, and it rises (Figure 9a). Cooler air from over the ocean moves in to replace it. The result is a wind that is commonly called an onshore breeze or sea breeze. Similarly, air heated by a fire in a fireplace rises, carrying smoke up a chimney rather than back into the house (Figure 9b).

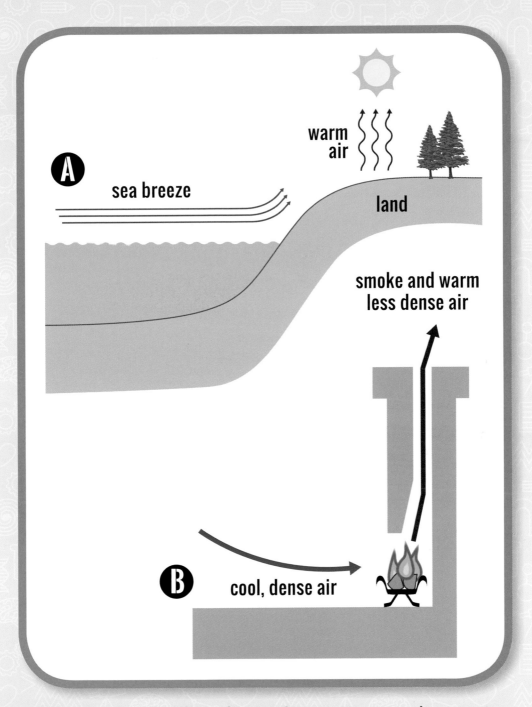

Figure 9. a) On a sunny day, cool air over the ocean moves in to replace warm air rising over land. b) Convection can take place in a chimney.

Design and carry out an experiment to show the difference in thermal conductivity of different metals. Use wires of different metals that have the same length and thickness.

Design and carry out an experiment to show how thermal conductivity depends on length and thickness using metal wires of the same material.

Compare the thermal conductivity of plastic, wood, glass, and different metals by timing how long identical ice cubes take to melt on surfaces of each. Kitchen cutting boards and pans can be used.

Chapter 4

Latent and Specific Heat

During his time experimenting with heat, Joseph Black noticed that ice and snow melt without any change in temperature. But when ice melted in his hands, Black could feel heat flowing from his hands into the ice. There is no change in the temperature of ice while it melts. Therefore, Black called the heat needed to melt ice its "latent heat of melting." ("Latent" means "hidden.") He called the heat that raises temperature "sensible heat."

Black realized that the earth is very fortunate that water has a latent heat of melting. He wrote, "Were the ice and snow to melt suddenly ... the torrents and inundations [floods] would be incomparably more irresistible and dreadful. They would tear up and sweep away everything."

To measure the heat required to melt ice, Black prepared two containers. One contained liquid water at 0°C (32°F). The other held an equal weight of ice at 0°C (32°F). He placed both containers in a room where the temperature remained at 48°F throughout the experiment. After 30 minutes, the temperature of the water had risen to 4.5°C (40°F). However, it was 10 hours later before the ice melted and reached a temperature of 4.5°C (40°F).

Black reasoned that both containers received the same amount of heat every hour. After all, the containers were in the same room and were about the same size. It took 10 1/2 hours to melt the ice and warm the meltwater to 4.5°C (40°F). The cold water had reached the same temperature in just 1/2 hour. If one unit of heat had warmed the cold water by -13°C (8°F), then twenty times as much heat was needed to melt the ice.

You can do an experiment similar to the one Joseph Black carried out 250 years ago, but you can measure the heat in calories.

4.1 Melting Ice

You can compare the heat needed to melt some ice with the heat needed to warm an equal mass of ice water through 10°C (18°F).

1. Pour 50 mL (50 g) of water into a graduated cylinder or a metric measuring cup.

2. Pour the 50 g of water into a clear plastic cup. Place the cup in a freezer. Leave it there overnight to be sure the water freezes completely.

3. The next day, add water to a 1-quart (1-L) plastic container until it is about half full. Then add ice cubes until it is about two-thirds full. Stir the mixture with a thermometer until it reaches 0°C (32°F). Remove any ice.

4. Record the time. Then quickly measure out 50 mL (50 g) of the ice water in a graduated cylinder or a metric measuring cup. Pour that water into another clear plastic cup. Put a thermometer in the water. How long does it take for the water temperature to rise to 10°C (50°F)? Record that time. How much heat, in calories, went into the water in this amount of time?

5. Next, remove the plastic cup that holds the ice from the freezer. When you begin to see a thin film of moisture on the ice, you know it is starting to melt and is at 0°C (32°F). Record the time.

6. Let the ice melt. Then let the meltwater warm up to 10°C (50°F). Record the time when the meltwater reaches this temperature. How long did it take for the ice to melt and warm by 10°C (18°F)?

   Assume that heat from the room went into the ice and the cold water at the same rate. How much heat, in calories, was needed to melt the 50 g of ice? How much heat was needed to melt 1 g of ice? How does your result compare to the accepted modern value of 80 calories per gram of ice?

4.2 Heat, Water, and Steam

When water reaches the boiling point (100°C or 212°F at sea level), it changes from a liquid to a gas (steam). But the temperature remains at 100°C (212°F) as it boils. Heat is needed to change one gram of water to a gas at the boiling temperature. That heat is called the latent heat of vaporization.

You can measure the latent heat of vaporization by doing an experiment. The experiment is similar to experiments done by early scientists.

1. Using a metric measuring cup, add exactly 300 mL (300 g) of water to a small cooking pan. Measure and record the water's temperature.

2. **Ask an adult** to heat the pan on a stove. Record the time when heating begins. **Put on safety glasses** in case the water spatters as it boils. Stir the water gently as it warms. Record the time again when the temperature stops rising and the water begins to boil.

3. Read the thermometer. Try to keep the thermometer bulb just above the bottom of the pan. (The metal pan will be hotter than the water.) Record the temperature at one-minute intervals. Do this for five minutes or until you are convinced that the temperature of the boiling water is remaining constant.

4. **Have the adult** continue to heat the pan until the water has completely or almost completely boiled away. Record the time when all the water has changed to gas.

Find the time it took to heat the water from its initial temperature to the boiling temperature. Let that time represent one unit of heat from the stove. How many units of heat did it take to boil away all the water? How many calories were needed to change one gram of water to steam?

For example, it may take six minutes to warm 300 g of water from 19°C to the boiling temperature (100°C at sea level). Another thirty minutes may be needed to boil away all the water. Therefore, it would take 5 times as much heat (30 × 6) to boil away the water as it would to raise its temperature by 81°C (100°C – 19°F C). In this example, one unit of heat raises the water's temperature by 81°C; five units of heat are needed to change the water to a gas.

One unit of heat in this experiment is:

300 g × 81°C = 24,300 calories.

Five units of heat would be:

5 × 24,300 calories = 121,500 calories.

The heat to boil away one gram would be:

121,500 cal/300g = 405 cal/g.

Design and, **under adult supervision**, carry out an experiment of your own to measure the heat needed to change one gram of steam at 100°C to water.

4.3 Cooking Oil and Heat Capacity

It takes one calorie to raise the temperature of one gram of water by one degree Celsius. How much heat do you think it would take to raise the temperature of one gram of cooking oil by one degree Celsius?

1. Pour 100 g of cooking oil into a foam cup. Since one milliliter of cooking oil weighs only 0.89 g, it will take 112 mL of cooking oil to weigh 100 grams.

2. Place the 112 mL of cooking oil in a refrigerator for at least one hour.

3. Near the end of the hour, measure 100 g (100 mL) of cold water in a graduated cylinder or a metric measuring cup. Pour that water into a foam cup.

4. Measure and record the temperature and mass of the cold water.

5. **Ask an adult** to put an immersion heater in the water (Figure 10) and plug the heater into an electrical outlet for exactly 30 seconds. After 30 seconds, **the adult** should unplug the heater. Leave the heater in the water so that all its heat can be transferred to the water.

6. Use the thermometer to stir the water. Record the temperature when it stops rising. This is the final temperature of the water. Record the water's change in temperature.

7. Calculate the heat, in calories, delivered by the immersion heater in 30 seconds.

8. Remove the cooking oil from the refrigerator. Stir it gently with the thermometer, then measure and record its temperature.

9. **Ask the adult** to put the immersion heater in the cooking oil and plug the heater into an electrical outlet for exactly 30 seconds. After 30 seconds, **the adult** should unplug the heater but leave it in the cooking oil.

10. Use the thermometer to stir the cooking oil. Record its final temperature. Record the change in temperature of the cooking oil. The immersion heater must have delivered the same amount of heat to the cooking oil as it did to the water. It was plugged in for the same

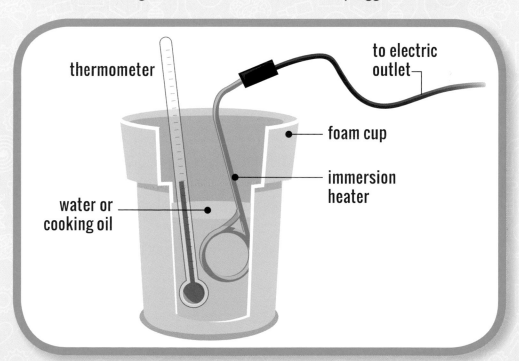

thermometer

to electric outlet

foam cup

immersion heater

water or cooking oil

Figure 10. Use an immersion heater to add heat to water and cooking oil.

amount of time. Therefore, how much heat, in calories, was delivered to the cooking oil?

What was the change in temperature of the cooking oil?

How much heat was needed to raise the temperature of 100 g of cooking oil by 1°C?

The heat needed to raise the temperature of any sample of matter by one degree Celsius is called its heat capacity. You have just found the heat capacity of a 100-g sample of cooking oil.

The heat capacity of a sample of matter depends on its mass. For example, to raise the temperature of 100 g of water by 1°C requires 100 calories. Therefore, the heat capacity of a 100-g sample of water would be 100 cal/°C. The heat capacity of 200 g of water would be 200 cal/°C. What would be the heat capacity of 200 g of cooking oil?

As you can see, the heat capacities of the same mass of water and cooking oil are different. Every substance has its own heat capacity. For convenience, scientists compare the heat capacities of 1 g of different substances.

The heat capacity of 1 g of a substance is called its "specific heat." Therefore, the specific heat of a substance is the amount of heat needed to raise the temperature of 1 g of the substance by 1°C. The specific heat of water is 1.0 (cal/g)/°C because it takes 1 calorie to raise the temperature of 1 g of water by 1°C.

The specific heat of any sample of matter is equal to its heat capacity divided by its mass in grams. For example, consider 100 g of water. It will take 100 calories to raise its temperature by 1°C. Its heat capacity is 100 cal/°C. Therefore, the specific heat of water is:

$$\frac{100 \text{ cal/}°C}{100 \text{ g}} = 1 \text{ (cal/}°C)/g, \text{ which is the same as } 1(\text{cal/g})/°C.$$

Use the data you have collected to calculate the specific heat of the cooking oil. For example, in one experiment, the data shown in Table 4 was obtained. According to this data, the heat capacity of the cooking oil was:

$$1{,}750 \text{ cal}/34.0°C = 51.5 \text{ cal/}°C.$$

The specific heat of the cooking oil was:
$$\frac{51.5 \text{ cal}/°C}{100 \text{ g}} = 0.515 \text{ (cal}/°C)/g.$$

How do your calculations of heat capacity and specific heat for cooking oil compare with these results?

In one experiment, Joseph Black mixed mercury at a temperature of 0°C with an equal mass of water at 20°C. (Remember, mercury is poisonous, so never experiment with it.) The temperature of the mixture was not 10°C. It was 19.4°C. Black had shown that different substances with the same mass have different heat capacities and different specific heats.

Assume Black used 100 g of both water and mercury in his experiment. The water gained:
$$100 \text{ g} \times (20°C - 19.4°C) = 100 \text{ g} \times 0.6°C = 60 \text{ calories.}$$

The mercury gained the 60 calories of heat that were lost by the water. The heat capacity of the 100 g of mercury was:
$$60 \text{ cal}/19.4°C = 3.1 \text{ cal}/°C.$$

Its specific heat according to Black's experiment was:
$$\frac{3.1 \text{ cal}/°C}{100 \text{ g}} = 0.031 \text{ (cal}/°C)/g.$$

TABLE 4

Sample Data Collected in Determining the Heat Capacity and Specific Heat of a Sample of Cooking Oil

	Water	Cooking Oil
Volume	100 mL	112 mL
Mass	100 g	100 g
Initial Temperature	2.5°C	5.0°C
Final Temperature	30.0°C	39.0°C
Temperature Change	17.5°C	34.0°C
Heat Gained	1,750 cal	1,750 cal

Under adult supervision, find the heat capacity and specific heat of a sample of ethylene glycol (the antifreeze used in cars).

Perform a mixing experiment like the one with mercury that Joseph Black performed to determine the specific heat of different solids. One way to do this is to put solids of known mass in a freezer. When they are cold they can be added to a known mass of warm water. Compare your results with the accepted modern values shown in Table 5.

TABLE 5
Specific Heats of Some Common Solids

Solid	Specific Heat (cal/°C/g)	Solid	Specific Heat (cal/°C/g)
Aluminum	0.22	Iron (Steel)	0.105
Brass	0.092	Lead	0.031
Copper	0.092	Magnesium	0.243
Glass	0.16	Silver	0.056
Gold	0.031	Zinc	0.092

Chapter 5

Temperature and Matter

What happens when you add heat to ice? You probably guess that the ice melts. But what happens to the temperature during the melting? When you add heat to ice, the temperature remains at 0°C (32°F) while the ice melts. This heat, which does not cause a temperature change, is the latent heat of melting. A question we might ask is, "Do all materials show a latent heat of melting?"

A cook will tell you that foods cook faster at a higher temperature. Cooking is one example of a chemical reaction. So another question might be, "Do other chemical reactions happen faster at a higher temperature?"

In this chapter you will explore these questions in three experiments. These experiments will not tell you everything about the effect of temperature on matter. It is unscientific to draw general conclusions from even several examples. However, the experiments may help you begin to think about other questions you might ask. And they may help you design experiments to answer the questions.

5.1 Getting Cool

In this experiment you will measure the temperature of two materials as they freeze—turn from liquid to solid. The first is water. The second is margarine. By making graphs of temperature versus time for both, you can investigate the freezing process in detail. This experiment will be much easier to do if you have access to a digital (electronic) thermometer. Inexpensive digital thermometers are available from all science supply companies (see appendix).

1. Fill a 12-oz (350-mL) foam cup two-thirds full with crushed ice or snow.

2. Add a few ounces of water and several tablespoons of rock salt. Stir vigorously with a stirring rod or the metal probe of the digital thermometer.

3. Measure the temperature. The temperature should drop to approximately -10°C (14°F).

4. Rinse the thermometer with tap water and fill a test tube halfway with warm tap water.

5. Insert the thermometer and measure the temperature of the warm water. Then immediately insert the test tube into the ice.

6. Let the test tube rest in the ice. Measure the temperature every thirty seconds for about ten minutes, or until it gets close to –10°C (14°F). Enter the times and temperature readings in a data table.

7. Plot a graph of temperature versus time, and connect your data with a smooth line. This shape is called a cooling curve.

    Describe the main features of the cooling curve. Are there any parts of the cooling curve that are surprising? Is there a part that might relate to the latent heat of melting?

8. Half fill a test tube with margarine. Melt the margarine by holding the test tube in a cup of hot tap water.

9. Repeat the experiment with the test tube in the ice.

10. Graph the cooling curve for margarine. Compare it to the one for water. Are there any differences?

Figures 11a and 11b show the cooling curves for water and margarine obtained by the author. How do they compare to yours? Did your results show the water dipping several degrees below 0°C before bouncing up to 0°C? This temporary dip is called supercooling. It does not always occur, especially if the water is disturbed as it cools.

Look at your cooling curve. Does it show the temperature holding steady at 0°C for a while before dropping to the ice-bath temperature? This is called the freezing plateau. It shows that the water is releasing heat as it freezes. Do you think the "freezing plateau" is related to the latent heat of melting? Does your margarine cooling curve have a freezing plateau? Would margarine have a latent heat of melting?

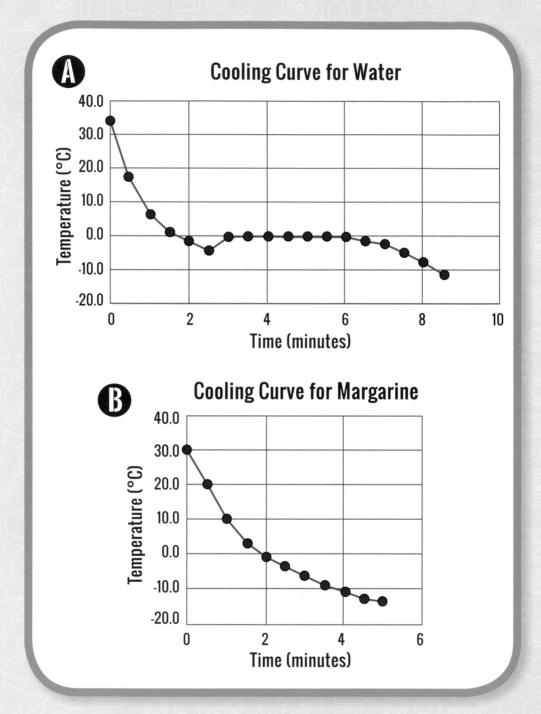

Figure 11. Cooling curves for a) water and b) margarine

Using a digital thermometer, design and do an experiment to compare the lowest temperature that can be obtained by mixing ice with different substances. For instance, compare ice in regular rock salt (sodium chloride), calcium chloride, potassium chloride, sugar, and ethylene glycol (antifreeze).

Design an experiment to compare the cooling curves of water that have different amounts of dissolved sugar. For instance, compare solutions that have 5 percent sugar (5 grams of sugar in 95 grams of water), 10 percent sugar, 15 percent sugar, and 20 percent sugar.

5.2 Temperature and Reaction Speed

THINGS YOU WILL NEED:

- clear 12-oz (350-mL) glass
- tap water
- lab thermometer (–10 to 110°C or 14 to 230°F) or digital thermometer
- at least 5 seltzer tablets
- watch or clock with second hand
- graph paper
- pen or pencil
- notebook

Foods cook faster at a higher temperature. But the outside may burn before the inside is cooked if the temperature is too high.

In this experiment, you will be making measurements to find a rule. The rule describes how temperature determines the time for seltzer tablets to completely dissolve in water. If you find a rule, you can use it to predict how long the process will take at different temperatures.

1. Fill a glass with tap water and measure its temperature. The temperature should be approximately 20°C (68°F).
2. Be sure your hands are dry. Then drop the first seltzer tablet into the water and begin timing.
3. When the tablet reaches the size of a dime and begins to be "eaten" all the way through, note the time in seconds.
4. Prepare a data table of water temperature and the time to dissolve.
5. Repeat steps 2 and 3 with fresh tap water at about 5°C, 10°C, 30°C, and 40°C (41°F, 50°F, 86°F, 104°F). You can get cool temperatures (5°C or 10°C [41°F or 50°F]) by cooling tap water with ice. Get warm water (30°C and 40°C[86°F or 104°F]) from the hot water tap.

6. Make a graph of dissolving time versus temperature. When the author performed this experiment, he obtained the graph shown in Figure 12. How do his results compare to yours?

   Do your data points fall along a smooth curve? Do your results follow a rule? For example, does it always take a certain increase in temperature to reduce the time by a certain amount? Or, does it always take the same increase in temperature to cut the dissolve time in half (no matter what the first temperature)?

7. Use your graph to predict the dissolving time for other temperatures. Then test your predictions.

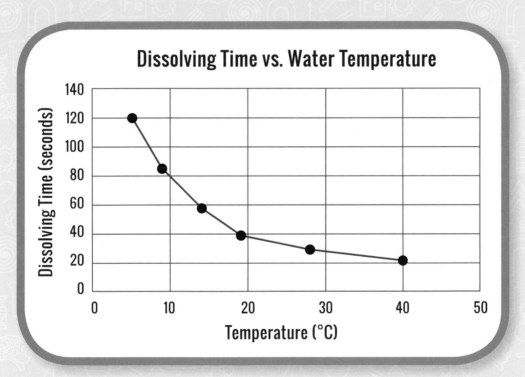

Figure 12. A graph of the time for a seltzer tablet to dissolve versus water temperature.

A seltzer tablet in water fizzes. This is the result of the reaction of its main ingredients—baking soda (sodium bicarbonate) and citric acid. Water dissolves these ingredients. They do not react when dry. One might think that temperature affects the speed of this reaction by increasing the rate that the tablets dissolve. Design and do an experiment to determine how the time required to dissolve sugar cubes or some other substance depends on water temperature.

Design an experiment to determine how the baking time of cupcakes is affected by temperature. What is the lowest temperature that will work? If the temperature is too high, what happens? **Have an adult** help you carry out this experiment.

5.3 Color and Temperature

When the heating element on an electric stove is set at high, it glows red. Objects begin to glow red (become "red hot") at about 600°C (1,100°F). As the temperature rises, the light gets brighter and changes color. By the time it reaches 1,000°C (1,800°F), it begins to turn yellow. By 1,500°C (2,700°F), the light is bright and yellow. This is the color of a campfire. By 2,500°C (4,500°F), the temperature reached in electric lightbulbs with tungsten filaments, the light becomes white.

In this experiment, you will observe these changing colors. You can do it by increasing the electric current in a flashlight bulb.

1. Carefully wrap 1.2m (4 ft) of Nichrome wire around a pencil to make a coil (see Figure 13).
2. Screw the flashlight bulb into the socket and insert the battery in the holder.
3. Connect one end of the Nichrome wire to one clip of the socket.
4. Connect the red lead from the battery holder to the other clip of the socket.

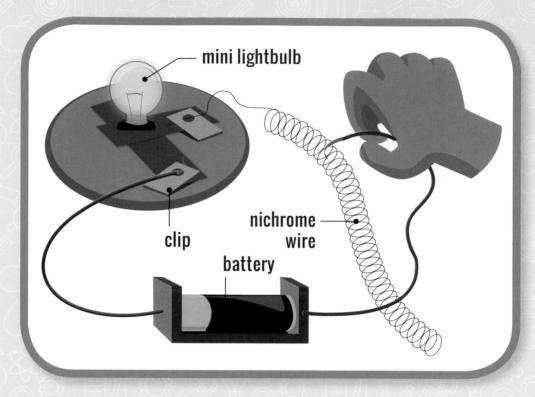

Figure 13. How is the color of a lightbulb's filament affected by temperature?

5. Turn off all the lights in the room except for a desk lamp above your work space.

6. Press the black lead from the battery holder to the clip where the Nichrome wire is attached. The lightbulb should glow fairly brightly with a yellow-white light.

7. Turn off the desk lamp. Begin touching the black battery lead to the Nichrome wire at different points along its length. The more wire you put in the circuit, the dimmer the bulb becomes. Adding more wire reduces the electric current that passes through the bulb.

8. Observe and record the color changes as the light grows dimmer. Give your eyes time to adjust to the darkness. A magnifying glass might help you see the colors better.

Just for Fun

You can determine the temperature of "red-hot" by performing a mixing experiment. **Have an adult** use tongs to heat an iron bolt in a flame until it is red-hot. Drop the hot bolt into a known mass of water in a ceramic coffee mug. Measure the temperature change. Iron has a specific heat of 0.105 (cal/°C)/g. Because heat is conserved, we can write an equation:

0.105 × mass of bolt × its temperature change = mass of water × its temperature change.

Using this equation, determine the temperature change of the bolt from the mass of the bolt, the mass of the water, and the temperature change of the water. Adding this temperature change to the starting temperature of the bolt (room temperature) will give you its hottest temperature. **Do this experiment under adult supervision.** Handling a red-hot bolt can be dangerous.

Optical pyrometers are instruments that match the color of an electric filament like those found in lightbulbs with the temperature found inside furnaces (red-hot or greater). Do some research on these devices.

Chapter 6

More Experiments About Heat

People rub their hands together when they are cold because rubbing things together causes heat. Rubbing two sticks together is another example; the friction can make them so hot that they burn.

Why does rubbing and banging things together make them warmer? According to the caloric theory of heat, an object becomes warmer when heat flows into it from a warmer object. But this does not seem to apply to rubbing. This exception may be a serious problem for the caloric theory.

In the following experiment, you will measure the heat that pieces of metal mixed with water generate when they are simply shaken inside a jar.

6.1. Making Heat

THINGS YOU WILL NEED:

- 109 grams of copper shot
- balance to measure mass
- water
- graduated cylinder
- 8-oz (230-mL) plastic jar with screw-on lid
- lab thermometer (-10°C to 110°C or 14 to 230°F) or digital thermometer
- watch or clock
- notebook
- pen or pencil

The heat capacities of 109 g of copper and 10 g of water are nearly the same. (Remember, heat capacity is the heat needed to change the temperature of a sample of matter by one degree Celsius.) You can prove this. Mix 109 g of cold copper shot and 10 g (10 mL) of hot water in a foam cup. Measure the final temperature. It will be halfway between the two extreme temperatures. Try it for yourself.

To find how much heat you can produce by shaking, you can do an experiment.

1. Add 109 grams of copper shot and 10 g of water to a plastic jar. Measure and record the temperature.

2. Screw on the lid. Hold the jar in front of you. Put both of your thumbs on the jar's lid and both sets of your middle three fingers on the jar's bottom. Shake the jar up and down for one minute.

3. Quickly open the jar. Measure and record the temperature.

4. Calculate the heat produced, in calories, by multiplying the temperature change by 20 g:

Heat produced by shaking = 20 g × temperature change.

84

This works because the 109 grams of copper has the same heat capacity as 10 grams of water. Therefore, the contents of the jar behave like 20 grams of water.

What temperature change did one minute of shaking cause? Could the heat have come from your hands? You can find out.

5. Measure the temperature of the copper and water. Then hold the jar in your hands in the same way for one minute, without shaking the jar. Measure the temperature again. What do you conclude?

6. Repeat the experiment with longer shaking periods. How do you think the temperature changes will depend on the shaking time?

7. Plot a graph of temperature rise versus shaking time. Are the results the same or different than you expected? If different, can you make a hypothesis about why and test it?

The Kinetic Theory of Heat

The caloric theory of heat explains the rules of temperature change and thermal expansion. But, as you have seen, the theory has problems. First, unlike other fluids, caloric seems to be weightless and invisible. Second, heat moves more easily through metals than gases. This is true even though there is more space between gas particles for it to move through. Finally, heat seems to be created from nothing by rubbing or shaking. This contradicts the idea that heat is conserved.

The fact that heat is produced when objects rub together led to a new theory of heat and temperature. This theory is known as the "kinetic theory." According to the kinetic theory, temperature is a side effect of the motions of the particles (atoms and molecules) that make up matter. While an object may be at rest, its atoms or molecules are always vibrating. The vibrations cannot be seen, but they can be felt. Gentle vibrations are felt as low temperature; rapid vibrations are felt as high temperature. Heat is just the motion of atoms and molecules.

According to the kinetic theory, when a solid object is rubbed or shaken, the motion does not really disappear when the shaking stops. Instead, the shaking causes the object's atoms or molecules to vibrate faster.

Benjamin Thompson (1753–1814), also known as Count Rumford, did not like the caloric theory. He was one of the first scientists to do experiments to support the kinetic theory. Born in Massachusetts, Thompson served as a British spy before fleeing to England at the start of the American Revolution. After serving as a British officer during the war, he moved to Bavaria (now part of Germany). While there, Thompson distinguished himself as a scientist, engineer, and inventor. He studied the insulating properties of clothing. He discovered convection. And he invented such practical items as the kitchen range, the double boiler, and the baking oven.

Thompson is famous for two series of experiments that challenged the caloric theory. In the first, using very precise scales, he carefully weighed objects as they cooled. The fact that they lost no mass convinced him that heat was not a real substance. Thompson's second series of experiments took place while he was in charge of the military arsenal in Munich, Germany. He used a cannon-boring machine (see Figure 14a) to grind a blunt iron borer against a hollowed iron cylinder. This rubbing produced enough heat to boil large amounts of water surrounding the machine. Since he had insulated the water, the large quantities of heat could not have been coming from the outside. The results, he argued, were better explained by the kinetic theory.

The kinetic theory is based on the idea that matter is made up of very small particles called atoms. The concept of atoms was first proposed by the Greek philosopher Democritus nearly 2,400 years ago. But it was not until Thompson's lifetime that scientists began to use the idea of atoms to explain many of the processes observed in nature.

Although early scientists could not see atoms, they could form mental images or models of them. Some of their early ideas turned out to be correct. Others required more than a century to fully develop.

Today, we know that substances made of only one type of atom are "elements." Iron, copper, carbon, and oxygen are examples of elements. Substances made by combining different atoms into molecules are called "compounds." An example of a compound is water. Each water molecule is made up of two hydrogen atoms joined to one oxygen atom (see Figure 14b).

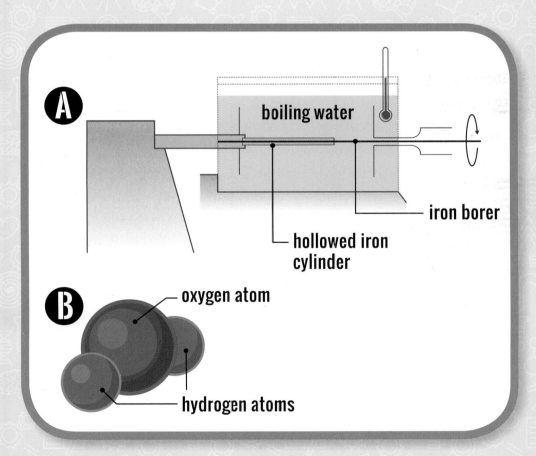

Figure 14. a) The canon-boring machine used by Benjamin Thompson
b) A drawing of a water molecule, greatly enlarged

6.2 **A Look at the Structure of Matter**

You have learned that matter can exist as solid, liquid, or gas, depending on the temperature. The state in which the matter exists depends on the way that atoms or molecules are joined together. In this experiment you will build a simple model of matter. You will use this model to explain the processes of melting, vaporization, thermal expansion, and conduction.

1. Place about 50 marbles in a tray with steep sides (or in a box). Tip the tray at an angle so that the marbles all collect at one end (see Figure 15). Notice how they line up in a definite pattern of straight rows. This arrangement of marbles represents the atoms (or molecules) in the solid state. The atoms are held together in their tightly packed and ordered arrangement by attractive forces called chemical bonds.

2. Keeping the tray tilted at the same angle, jiggle it gently but rapidly. Notice how the marbles vibrate while staying in the same ordered arrangement. This condition of the model represents a solid at a higher temperature. The jiggling marbles represent vibrating atoms or molecules. The faster their vibrations, the higher the temperature will be. Notice that the marbles take up slightly more space when they are jiggling. This illustrates thermal expansion.

3. Now, decrease the tilt of the tray to a very small angle. Gradually increase the amount of jiggling. Notice how the marbles no longer stay in their ordered rows. Even though they are still grouped together, they change positions, leaving small open spaces between them. Also, as you turn the tray, the marbles "flow" as a group. This condition of the model represents a liquid.

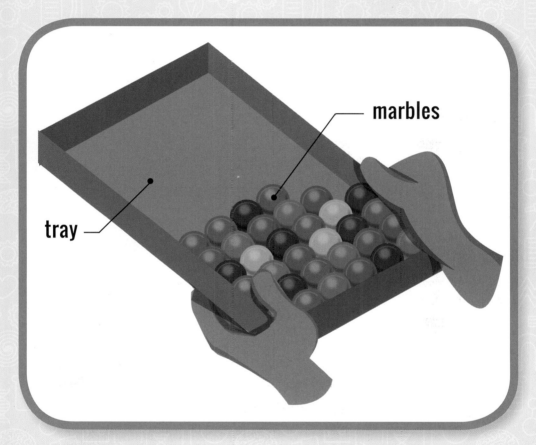

marbles

tray

Figure 15. A model, based on the kinetic theory, represents the solid state of matter.

4. Next, place the tray on a flat surface. Shake it vigorously. Notice how the marbles fill the entire tray, bouncing off each other and the tray's walls in a chaotic manner. The marbles no longer

jiggle. They "fly" in straight lines until they bump into other marbles or the walls of the tray. This condition of the model represents a gas. Vigorous shaking in our model corresponds to high temperature in the atomic world. At a high temperature, the vibrations are so large that the atoms or molecules separate. They become a gas.

- Design and build your own model to show how temperature affects matter on a molecular level.

- Design and build a model to show how temperature affects the volume of a gas on a molecular level.

- Design and build a model to show how pressure affects the volume of a gas on a molecular level.

6.3. A Simple Air Thermometer

THINGS YOU WILL NEED:

- modeling clay
- plastic drinking straw
- 15-cm ruler
- clear tape
- green food coloring
- eyedropper
- tablespoon
- tap water (cold, cool, and warm)
- 3 clear, tall glasses
- ice cubes
- lab thermometer (–10 to 110°C or 14 to 230°F) or digital thermometer
- notebook
- pen or pencil
- graph paper

One prediction of the kinetic theory of heat is that there must be a lowest temperature. This is simply the temperature at which atomic vibrations stop. This idea was fully explained by the Scottish physicist James Clerk Maxwell (1831–1879).

Maxwell was not the first to think of the possibility of a lowest temperature. In 1702, French scientist Guillaume Amontons (1663–1705) came up with the idea while experimenting with an air thermometer. This thermometer was an air-filled glass tube. It was sealed at the bottom and plugged at the top by a small drop of mercury. The mercury was free to move up and down (Figure 16a). As the temperature of the surroundings decreased, the air trapped inside contracted (shrank). Amontons was not thinking about the kinetic theory of heat. Nevertheless, he believed that the lowest possible temperature would be reached when the air's volume shrank to zero.

In this experiment you will construct a simple air thermometer and use it to estimate the lowest temperature in degrees Celsius.

1. Push a small amount of clay into the bottom of a plastic straw. Add a little more around the outside of the bottom to seal it (Figure 16b).

2. Line up the 0-cm line of a ruler with the top of the clay pushed into the bottom of the straw. Using small pieces of clear tape, attach the ruler to the side of the straw.

3. Add a drop of green food coloring to a tablespoon of water and fill the eyedropper.

4. Fill one tall glass halfway with cold water. Add ice until the glass is full. Fill a second glass with cool tap water. Fill a third with very hot tap water.

5. Put the thermometer in the hot water glass. Then put the straw and attached ruler in the hot water. Its top should be about 1 cm above the waterline. Using the eyedropper, carefully insert a couple of drops of colored water into the top of the straw to form a water "plug." The plug will trap the warm air inside the straw.

6. Record the temperature of the hot water and the level of the bottom of the water plug. The diameter of the straw is fixed, so the plug level is a measure of the volume of the trapped air.

7. Move the thermometer and straw into the cool water. The water plug should drop as the cooling air contracts. When it settles into a new steady position, record the new temperature and the new plug level.

8. Finally, move the thermometer and straw into the ice water. When the water plug settles to its new lower level, record the temperature and plug level.

9. Remove the straw. Record the three plug levels that go with the three temperatures. Make a data table of the temperatures and plug levels.

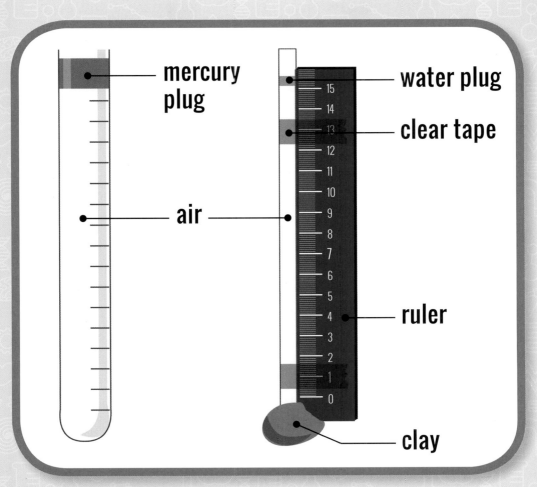

Figure 16. a) A drawing shows Amontons's air thermometer. b) You can make an air thermometer.

10. Make a graph with temperature on the horizontal axis and plug level on the vertical axis. Set the range of the plug level axis from 0 cm to just above the plug level for the hot water. Set the range of the temperature axis from –300°C to 50°C.

11. Draw a straight line that passes through your three data points and continues all the way to the bottom of the graph (to a volume of 0). The temperature at which it crosses the 0-cm level is the lowest temperature. It is the temperature at which the air's volume would be zero.

What is the lowest temperature you found? How does it compare with the lowest temperature that the author obtained, as shown in Figure 17?

British physicist William Thomson (1824–1907) added to this better understanding of the lowest temperature. (For his scientific work, Thomson was honored with the title of Lord Kelvin.) This lowest possible temperature, called "absolute zero," was measured in his day to be –273°C (–459.4°F). The more precise modern value is –273.15°C (–459.67°F).

In honor of Lord Kelvin, the modern absolute temperature scale is named the Kelvin scale. It assigns 0 kelvin (K) to the lowest temperature and uses units equal in size to 1°C. Therefore, on the Kelvin scale water freezes at 273.15 K and boils at 373.15 K.

The Triumph of the Kinetic Theory

According to the kinetic theory of heat, heat is not a substance. Rather, it is a property of vibrating atoms and molecules. According to this theory, temperature is not a measure of the crowdedness of caloric fluid. Instead, temperature is related to the speed of vibrating atoms or molecules.

We have seen that this theory can explain melting and vaporization, the lowest temperature, and thermal expansion. Can it also explain the rules of temperature change, thermal conduction, and why seltzer reacts faster in hot water than in cold? Can it explain why cookies bake faster at a high temperature than at a low one? Unless a theory can explain at least everything that an old theory can, there is no reason to accept it.

Before reading the following explanations, try using the kinetic theory and your imagination to explain these rules and processes on your own. This is a good chance to think like a scientist. Write down your ideas in your notebook. Then compare your explanations with the ones given below.

Kinetic Theory and Conduction

When the tip of a solid rod is placed in a flame, the atoms in the tip vibrate faster. These faster-moving atoms bump into the neighboring atoms farther along the rod, making them vibrate faster too. These atoms, in

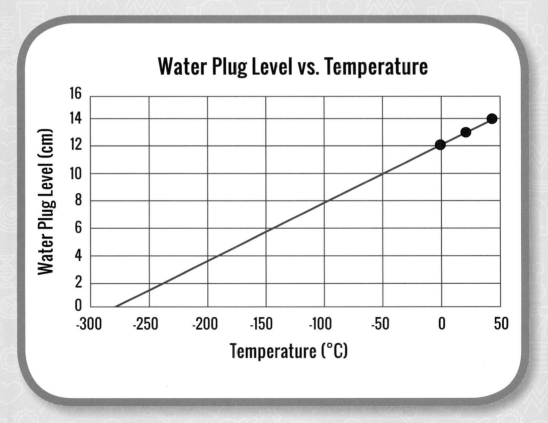

Figure 17. A graph of the author's results for Experiment 6.3 is shown.

turn, bump into atoms farther down the rod, and so on. As a result, the faster vibrations are soon transferred down the entire length of the rod. Heat conduction is this sharing of motion. More motion results in higher temperature.

Thermal conduction is caused by atoms passing their vibrations to neighboring atoms. Therefore, dense substances, such as metals, should conduct heat better than gases. After all, the atoms of dense matter are close together. The atoms of gases, on the other hand, are far apart. Gaseous atoms rely on collisions between distant atoms to transfer faster motion from one part of the gas to another.

Kinetic Theory and the Rules of Temperature Change

Recall the three rules of temperature change:

(1) When objects at different temperatures are in contact, the cooler one gets warmer and the warmer one gets cooler until their temperatures are equal.

(2) The greater the difference in temperature between two objects in contact, the faster their temperatures change.

(3) The greater the amount of something, the greater the temperature change it can cause in another object, and the less its own temperature changes in the process.

These rules can be explained as follows:

Rule 1: When two objects are touching, their vibrating atoms bump against each other. In this way, the atoms of a hot object conduct their greater speed to the atoms of the cooler object. The result is that the warm body cools and the cooler body warms. This transfer of atomic vibrations continues until the atoms in both bodies reach the same degree of atomic vibration (the same temperature).

Rule 2: The greater the difference in atomic vibrations, the faster they are transferred to the cooler object. To understand why, imagine a line of people with their hands joined. If the end person pulls or pushes gently, his or her neighbor will not move very fast. Therefore, the increased motion will be transferred along the line very slowly. However, if the end person pulls and pushes with a large force, the person pushed will acquire a greater speed. Therefore, that person will collide sooner with the next person. The same will hold for the next collision and so on all the way down the line.

Rule 3: A large object has many more vibrating atoms than a small one. When they are in contact, a small decrease in the vibration of the larger object's many atoms can add up to a large increase in the vibration of the small object's atoms. This motion causes a large temperature increase in the small object without much effect on the large object.

6.4 Heat Movement and Kinetic Theory

> ## THINGS YOU WILL NEED:
> - grooved one-foot ruler
> - table
> - 6 or 7 identical marbles or steel balls

To illustrate how heat moves according to the kinetic theory, you can do an experiment.

1. Place a grooved one-foot ruler on a table.
2. Place six or seven identical marbles side-by-side on the ruler, as shown in Figure 18. The marbles represent a few atoms in a solid, such as iron.
3. Pull one marble to the side. Give it a push. It will gain some speed. (An atom in contact with a flame will also gain vibrational speed.)

   When it hits the next marble, what happens?

How does this illustration model the way heat travels through a solid? How is it different?

Temperature and Chemistry

What happens at the atomic scale when seltzer reacts in water or when cookies bake? A more general question that includes these particular processes is, what is a chemical reaction?

According to the atomic/molecular model of matter, a chemical reaction is simply a rearrangement of atoms. The molecules of the starting substances break apart into atoms. Then these free atoms recombine in new ways to make the final molecules. For instance, when a seltzer tablet (containing sodium bicarbonate and citric acid) reacts in water, hydrogen atoms break free from the citric acid.

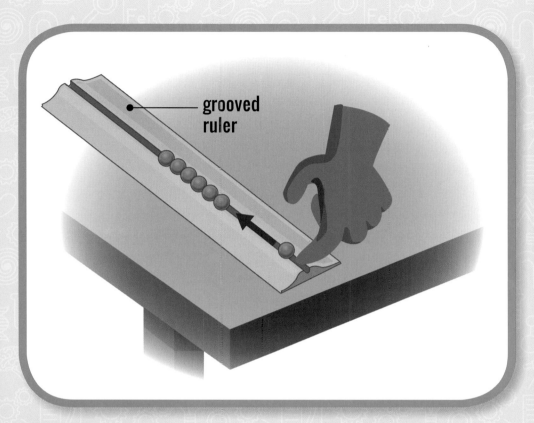

grooved
ruler

Figure 18. A model shows how heat travels according to the kinetic theory.

The carbon, sodium, and oxygen atoms also break free from the sodium bicarbonate. The hydrogen atoms recombine with some of the oxygen atoms to make water, and the rest of the carbon and oxygen atoms re-form as carbon dioxide molecules. The sodium atoms combine with what is left of the citric acid to form sodium citrate. The reaction can be represented by a chemical equation:

$$3NaHCO_3 + C_6H_8O_7 \rightarrow Na_3C_6H_5O_7 + 3CO_2 + 3H_2O.$$
sodium bicarbonate + citric acid $\rightarrow$ sodium citrate + carbon dioxide + water

The equation tells you that three molecules of sodium bicarbonate react with one molecule of citric acid to form one molecule of sodium citrate, three molecules of carbon dioxide, and three molecules of water.

Count the atoms of each element on both sides of the arrow. You will see they are equal in number. (Matter cannot be created or destroyed.)

Even though this example is a bit complicated, the basic idea is simple. For a reaction to occur, the molecules must be broken apart. What will cause this to happen? The molecules have to be moving fast so that they collide with great force. According to the kinetic theory, faster motion is caused by higher temperature.

The kinetic theory clearly explains why reactions happen faster at a higher temperature. In fact, one of James Clerk Maxwell's accomplishments was to show that increasing the temperature by 10°C will approximately double a reaction rate. Is that what you found in Experiment 5.2?

Conclusion

In this book you learned that thermometers provide a way of measuring temperature. You used thermometers to establish some rules of temperature change. And you used them to find out how heat differs from temperature.

You also learned that Joseph Black and Antoine Lavoisier developed a theory that explained the rules of temperature change. Their fluid (caloric) theory of heat successfully explained some properties of heat. However, further investigations revealed new facts about heat. It became clear that the fluid theory was flawed. First, it asked people to accept the idea of a weightless and invisible substance. Second, it was unable to explain why solids are better conductors of heat than gases. Finally, it failed to explain, as Benjamin Thompson's cannon-boring experiments showed, heating by rubbing.

According to the kinetic theory, temperature is a measurement of the average speed of atoms or molecules. Heat is to be found in the total motion of all these particles. The kinetic theory has been successful. It can explain temperature and heat without the need of an invisible, weightless fluid.

However, even though heat is not really a fluid, this does not mean that the fluid theory must be discarded. A story does not have to be true to teach a valuable lesson.

Similarly, a theory does not have to be perfect to be useful. In fact, modern scientists and engineers routinely use the fluid theory of heat. They talk about heat flowing from place to place as if it were a fluid. Only in cases in which the fluid theory does not adequately describe an observation does the kinetic theory become necessary.

Appendix

Science Supply Companies

Arbor Scientific
PO Box 2750
Ann Arbor, MI 48106-2750
(800) 367-6695
arborsci.com

Carolina Biological Supply Co.
PO Box 6010
Burlington, NC 27215-3398
(800) 334-5551
carolina.com

Connecticut Valley Biological
   Supply Co., Inc.
82 Valley Road
PO Box 326
Southampton, MA 01073
(800) 628-7748
ctvalleybio.com

Educational Innovations, Inc.
5 Francis J. Clarke Circle
Bethel, CT 06801
(203) 748-3224
teachersource.com

Fisher Science Education
300 Industry Drive
Pittsburgh, PA 15275
(800) 955-1177
fishersci.com

Frey Scientific
80 Northwest Blvd.
Nashua, NH 03061-3000
(800) 225-3739
freyscientific.com

Nasco
901 Janesville Ave.
Fort Atkinson, WI 53538
(800) 558-9595
enasco.com/science

Scientifics Direct
532 Main Street
Tonawanda, NY 14150
(800) 818-4955
scientificsonline.com

Ward's Science
5100 West Henrietta Road
PO Box 92912
Rochester, NY 14692-9012
(800) 962-2660
wardsci.com

Glossary

atomic theory The theory that matter is made up of very small particles called atoms.

caloric theory The theory that temperature measures how crowded the heat fluid is in an object.

calorie The quantity of heat gained or lost when one gram of water changes its temperature by 1°C.

capacity The heat needed to raise the temperature of any sample of matter by one degree Celsius.

Celsius temperature scale A temperature scale that defines the freezing temperature of water as 0°C and the boiling point of water as 100°C.

chemical compounds Substances consisting of two or more elements that are chemically joined.

chemical reaction A rearrangement of atoms that takes places when the molecules of the starting substances break apart into atoms. These free atoms recombine in new ways to form the final molecules.

conservation of heat A law of nature that states that heat is never lost. It may move from one object to another, but the heat lost by one object is gained by another object or objects.

conservation of matter A law of nature that states that matter cannot be created or destroyed.

convection The movement of heat due to differences in the density of the substances that carry the heat.

element A substance that cannot be separated into simpler substances, and has only one kind of atom.

Fahrenheit temperature scale A temperature scale that defines the freezing point of water as 32°F and the boiling point of water as 212°F.

kinetic theory The theory that heat is simply the motion of the atoms and molecules that make up matter. Temperature is a measure of the average speed of these atoms and molecules.

latent heat The heat absorbed or released during a change of state in which there is no change in temperature during the process.

latent heat of melting The heat needed to change one gram of solid to liquid at the melting temperature.

latent heat of vaporization The heat needed to change one gram of water to a gas at the boiling temperature.

laws of nature Rules that allow us to predict what will happen when certain conditions exist.

molecule One or more atoms of the discrete particles that make up a pure substance (an element or compound).

specific heat The heat capacity of one gram of a substance, or the amount of heat needed to raise the temperature of one gram of the substance by 1°C.

temperature A measure of the hotness or coldness of something.

theory An explanation that accounts for the laws of nature. The best theories explain many laws of nature and may even predict new ones.

thermal conductivity (heat conduction) The movement or flow of heat along or through a substance.

thermal conductors Substances that conduct heat well.

thermal expansion An increase in volume due to increasing temperature.

thermal insulators Substances that do not conduct heat well.

thermometer A device used to measure temperature.

Further Reading

Books

Ardley, Neil. *101 Great Science Experiments*. New York, NY: DK Ltd., 2014.

Brown, Jordan. *Science Stunts: Fun Feats of Physics*. Watertown, MA: Charlesbridge Publishing, 2016.

Buczynski, Sandy. *Designing a Winning Science Fair Project*. Ann Arbor, MI: Cherry Lake Publishing, 2014.

Henneberg, Susan. *Creating Science Fair Projects with Cool New Digital Tools*. New York, NY: Rosen Central, 2014.

Kenney, Karen Latchana. *The Science of Music: Discovering Sound*. Minneapolis, MN: ABDO Publishing, 2016.

Larson, Kirsten W. *Science Fair Success!* North Mankato, MN: Rourke Educational Media, 2015.

Mercer, Bobby. *Junk Drawer Physics: 50 Awesome Experiments That Don't Cost a Thing*. Chicago, IL: Chicago Review Press, Inc., 2014.

Rompella, Natalie. *Experiments in Material and Matter with Toys and Everyday Stuff*. North Mankato, MN: Capstone Press, 2016.

Websites

Exploratorium
exploratorium.edu/xref/phenomena/heat.html
Check out the Physics/Heat & Temperature experiments from the Teacher Institute at the Exploratorium.

NeoK12
neok12.com/Heat-Temperature.htm
Educational videos and games for students about heat and temperature.

Index

T

W

Robert Gardner is an award-winning author of science books for young readers. He retired from Salisbury School in Connecticut, where he chaired the science department for more than thirty years, to pursue a career as an author. He lives on Cape Cod with his wife, Patsy, and enjoys writing, biking, and doing volunteer work.